Safety Basics

by Rebecca Weber

CAPSTONE PRESS
a capstone imprint

Pebble Plus is published by Capstone Press,
1710 Roe Crest Drive, North Mankato, Minnesota 56003.
www.capstonepub.com

Books published by Capstone Press are manufactured with paper
containing at least 10 percent post-consumer waste.

Library of Congress Cataloging-in-Publication Data
Weber, Rebecca.
  Safety basics / by Rebecca Weber.
    p. cm. — (Pebble plus. Health and your body)
  Includes bibliographical references and index.
  Summary: "Color photos and simple text describe safety tips for home, school, and travel"—Provided by publisher.
  ISBN 978-1-4296-7694-6 (library binding) — ISBN 978-1-4296-7905-3 (paperback)
  1. Accidents—Prevention—Juvenile literature. 2. Personal injuries—Prevention—Juvenile literature. 3. Safety
    education—Juvenile literature. 4. Children—Life skills guides—Juvenile literature. I. Title.
  HV675.5.W435 2012
  613.6—dc23   2011029914

Editorial Credits
Gillia Olson, editor; Juliette Peters, designer; Wanda Winch, media researcher; Sarah Schuette, photo stylist;
    Marcy Morin, studio scheduler; Kathy McColley, production specialist

Photo Credits
All images by Capstone Studio: Karon Dubke

Note to Parents and Teachers

The Health and Your Body series supports national science standards related to health and physical
education. This book describes and illustrates basic safety practices. The images support early
readers in understanding the text. The repetition of words and phrases helps early readers learn
new words. This book also introduces early readers to subject-specific vocabulary words, which are
defined in the Glossary section. Early readers may need assistance to read some words and to use
the Table of Contents, Glossary, Read More, Internet Sites, and Index sections of the book.

Printed in the United States of America in North Mankato, Minnesota.
102011
006405CGS12

Table of Contents

How to Stay Safe

Follow a few simple tips to be safe at home, at school, and on the playground. The first tip is to think before you act. Could you or others get hurt?

At Home

Think about safety at home.

Cleaners and medicines

may be dangerous.

Always ask a parent

before touching those items.

Make your home a safe place.
Go through the house
with a parent. Label anything
that might be poisonous.
Get rid of old medicines.

9

At School

Follow the rules at school too.

Don't run in the halls.

Watch for slippery floors.

On a field trip, stay with the group so you don't get lost.

Strangers

Never go anywhere with
an adult you do not know.
Tell a parent or other
trusted adult right away
if a stranger approaches you.

Traveling

Be safe when you travel. In a car or truck, wear a seat belt. While walking or riding a bike, watch for cars. Always wear a helmet while biking.

Bus Safety

Practice safety on the bus. Stay in your seat when the bus is moving. When you get off the bus, always look for cars before crossing the road.

Playgrounds

Use playground equipment how it is meant to be used. Don't jump off climbers or stand on swings. Rules help you have fun without getting hurt.

Fire Safety at Home

Every home should have a plan in case of fire. You can make a plan and practice a fire drill at home.

1. Figure out two ways you can escape from your home.

2. Plan where everyone in the family will meet when they are outside the building.

3. Know what telephone numbers you should call for help once you are safe.

4. Practice the fire drill. See how long it takes everyone to get out safely. Practice until everyone knows what to do.

1.

2.

3.

Emergency Numbers

Police/Fire 911
Mom (cell) 555-4645
Dad (cell) 555-1777
Grandma Daisy 555-3070
Uncle Rob 555-3030
Neighbor Jane 555-6370

4.

OSLO

8:33:00

Glossary

approach—to come near someone on purpose, often to talk to the person

helmet—a hard hat that protects the head

poisonous—able to harm or kill

travel—to go from one place to another; to take a trip

trusted adult—a grown-up you know who is honest and who you can count on; trusted adults include your parents, teachers, and police officers

Read More

Donahue, Jill Urban. *Ride Right: Bicycle Safety.* How to Be Safe! Minneapolis: Picture Window Books, 2009.

Mara, Wil. *What Should I Do? Near a Busy Street.* Community Connections. Ann Arbor, Mich.: Cherry Lake Pub., 2011.

Rau, Dana Meachan. *School Safety.* Safe Kids. New York: Marshall Cavendish Benchmark, 2010.

Internet Sites

FactHound offers a safe, fun way to find Internet sites related to this book. All of the sites on FactHound have been researched by our staff.

Here's all you do:

Visit *www.facthound.com*

Type in this code: 9781429676946

Super-cool stuff! Check out projects, games and lots more at www.capstonekids.com

Index

Word Count: 209
Grade: 1
Early-Intervention Level: 21